WITCHES, WIZARDS AND WARLOCKS OF London

First published in 2003 by Watling St Publishing

The Glen

Southrop

Lechlade

Gloucestershire

GL7 3NY

Printed in Italy

ISBN 1-904153-12-7

24681097531

Design: Maya Currell
Cover design and illustration: Mark Davis
Cartoons: Martin Angel

WITCHES, WIZARDS AND WARLOCKS OF LONDON

Natasha Narayan

Natasha Narayan has worked as a journalist in Albania, Bosnia and Georgia and the former Soviet Union. She was also briefly education correspondent on the *Observer*, a waitress and a satellite TV presenter. She lives in North London with her husband, daughter and son.

For Nina with love.

Contents

Introduction   7

1 Waxy Witches   13

2 Cats, Bats, Rats and Other
  Nasty Pets   21

3 Witches in the Palace   28

4 Mirror, Mirror   40

5 Hubble Bubble, Spells
  and Potions   53

6 Witchfinders   59

7 Hex the Hag — Or How to Protect
  Yourself from Witchery   69

8 Nine of the Devil?   74

9 Hellish Nell   82

Witch Wisdom:
Test Your Knowledge   92

How to spot a wicked witch, weird wizard or warty warlock

You're on the bus to school – on a top-secret mission.

Reliable information has reached you that someone on the bus sups with the Devil; one of the innocent-looking people slouching on a seat near you is a witch, a wizard or a warlock.

Your eyes roam over the candidates. Hmm. Opposite you is an old woman with a crooked nose. Growing on the end of her nose is a big mole sprouting three ugly hairs. She is wearing an old black coat (or is it really a cloak?). And that umbrella she's carrying, is it in fact a broomstick?

But no, surely the old woman is too obvious. The witch is far more likely to be the woman next to her in a denim miniskirt and Nike trainers. Those trainers would be great when she goes flying off to meet her demon boyfriend.

Or what about the man sitting next to you? His hands and arms are thickly covered in a blanket of scratchy red hair. You can see the hairs poking through his shirt. Perhaps he has already begun his transformation into a wolf, and is only waiting for the full moon to go the full monty!

But hold on a second! What about the sleek-looking man behind you in a shiny purple jacket? He's carrying a heavy bag of books. Perhaps they contain his spellbooks of potions and necromancy!

The frustrating thing is, it's almost impossible to spot a witch – or a wizard – or a warlock – or even a werewolf, for that matter.

And if it's tough for you who have advantages (hot baths and electricity and proper schools, though the last may not seem much of an advantage), how much more trying for a Londoner in the Middle Ages?

Imagine for a moment that you're a medieval peasant. If you really want to get into it you will need to follow these simple steps:

1. Forgo baths for at least a month

2. Eat black bread and lard

3. Poo in the corner of your room

4. Cut up a smelly old blanket to wear as a coat

Witches and demons and malign flying beings are everywhere. The scary thing, the absolutely terrifying thing, in fact, is that you don't know who the witches are. It could be anyone. Smooth words and the smartest clothes can conceal the Devil's mark. Even the the Church is not above suspicion; after all, the Londoner Canon Southwell was found to be a wizard who practised black masses in the sixteenth century.

The most likely candidates for witches were the wizened old women who lived poor, lonely lives. But the young and pretty and the middle-aged and married could be witches too. Joan Waterhouse in Essex on the outskirts of London was only eighteen when she was tried for witchcraft in the sixteenth century.

In the bad times – and much of the Middle Ages were bad times, thanks to rotten food and yucky diseases like the plague – almost anybody could be attacked as a witch or wizard.

Little wonder that across Europe from 1400 to 1700 between 100,000 and 300,000 witches and wizards were put to death – often burnt at the stake after suffering the most hideous tortures.

And, it has to be said, that the ones tossed on the barbie were usually witches, not wizards.

In fact, some historians have suggested that the whole witch-craze thing was a way of cutting women down to size. The men didn't want their women to get too uppity and start demanding new–fangled 'rights'. Like the right not to bring their husbands a flagon of ale everytime they shouted for one. Or the right to their own opinions.

Here in London we were a bit kinder than the rest of Europe. We didn't usually burn witches. Just hanged them or cut off their heads – and we took a little bit more trouble to prove that they had done something wrong.

We don't know how many exactly were killed in and around London (there wasn't always a helpful newspaper reporter on hand when the witches were hanged) but the numbers run into hundreds.

Some of them were definitely harmless.

But on the other hand, very, very strange things did happen. Historical events that can't simply be explained by reason and science.

You might think that spells and enchantments, witches and wizards only happen in the pages of storybooks. But that's not the whole story. The witches and spells in this book are real.

There *was* a Philosopher's Stone. And there *were* powerful sorcerers who searched for the secret of turning metal into gold.

In fact history is full of spooky things, things that the Church and the Law couldn't control at all.

Put it this way: if you were a powerful witch who could transform yourself into a cat or fly hundreds of miles on a broomstick, would you let yourself meekly be tied to the stake and roasted by some bloke with NO MAGICAL POWERS at all?

Think about it. And think again. My guess is that most of the time the Law got the wrong people – or maybe they could only find the trainee witches. The ones who didn't really know their cauldrons from their broomsticks.

Indeed sometimes calling someone a witch was simply a good way of getting rid of a wife you'd tired of. Ask Henry VIII. He accused his second wife Anne Boleyn of witchcraft. Shortly afterwards she was toast (or at least her head was chopped off).

So thank the Lord that you live in the twenty-first century and not the super-spooky Witching Times ... when you too could easily be next in line for the hangman's noose.

CHAPTER ONE

Waxy Witches

Back in the mists of time when unicorns and wild beasts haunted London, witches and wizards were as common a nuisance on the streets as takeaway cartons are today.

Merlin, the super-magician, wise counsellor of King Arthur and his Knights of the Round Table, was rumoured to have learned his trade in London.

Indeed some historians believe that what the Christians condemned as evil trading with the Devil was just a hangover from the pagan beliefs and rituals of our Celtic ancestors.

Even by the tenth century, a thousand years after the birth of Christ, paganism was still going strong. (The pagan druids are the ones that wore white smocks and flowers in their hair and danced around big stones at full moon – a bit like hippies, really!)

Some sceptics think that witches and wizards never really existed and that all those poor people were barbied for nothing at all. Other historians think there may have been large groups of witches.

The whole subject is wrapped in mystery. The problem is that these witches and wizards – and the odd warty-weirdy warlock – didn't keep diaries.

In fact the earliest record of witchcraft we have in London dates from the late 900s. A woman and her son were tried for fashioning a clay image of a man and driving stakes into it (doesn't sound very friendly, does it?). They were taken and dropped off London Bridge. The woman drowned but the son managed to escape – presumably he knew how to swim.

Skipping a few centuries (to 1430 to be exact) we come to the first tale of a real witch.

Margery Jourdemaine was called the Witch of Eye – not because of her funny eyes but because she lived in the manor of Eye-Next-Westminster. Margery was a poor woman who made her living selling spells and potions. She treated people who often had more faith in 'cunning folk' and witches than doctors. They turned to charms and magic to cure even simple colds and fevers.

If Marge had stuck to her social circle – the labourers who lived in the narrow, reeking lanes of Westminster – we would never have heard of her. But she was good at magic and as her fame spread she was consulted by the poshest lords and ladies in the realm.

Her reputation for witchcraft first got her into hot water in 1430, when she was arrested, along with two clergymen, and imprisoned in Windsor Castle. But the case was dismissed and Margery was released.

However Marge's trouble really began when she was consulted by the Duchess of Gloucester, Lady Eleanor Cobham. Lady Eleanor is first said to have called on Marge to make her a love potion that would make her future husband – the Duke – infatuated with her.

Later Margery became involved – along with Lady Eleanor, the famous wizard Roger Bolingbroke and a clergyman, Canon Thomas Southwell – in a far more wicked plot.

They were accused of plotting to kill King Henry VI. Margery was accused of fashioning a wax figure of the king. The clergyman was to say a black mass in Hornsey Park – this was not an ordinary mass but a devilish version of the usual rite where often all the words were said backwards. Finally, the sorcerer Bolingbroke, with all his apparatus of conjuring and necromancy, was to tie it all together ... at least that is what we deduce.

But the plotters themselves denied any intent to kill the king. The duchess said that she was merely trying to conceive a child and the little wax figure was of the baby she so wanted.

In any event nobody believed them. Canon Southwell was lucky, in that he died in prison. Margery was taken to Smithfield and burnt as a witch. Roger Bolingbroke was hung, drawn and quartered – that means his body was literally cut into four pieces. His head was stuck on the gatehouse of London Bridge and bits of his body were sent to four different counties where they were put on public display.

And what of the wicked Duchess who had concocted the whole plot?

As you might have guessed, there was no public

burning or chopping for her. After all, she was dead posh! Instead she was made to walk around saying sorry and was later banished from London – which must have been a fate worse than death in the fifteenth century for a fashionable lady!

LONDON WITCH WATCH

Name: Elizabeth Barton, a nun, nicknamed 'The Holy Maid of Kent'.

Witchery: Barton, like Joan of Arc, claimed to hear angelic voices. The voices told her that King Henry VIII should not marry Anne Boleyn. The Virgin Mary also gave her a letter written in gold in heaven. But King Henry did not like her interference in his affairs.

Verdict: Hanged as a witch at Tyburn in 1534.

Weird Waxworks

Forget Madame Tussaud's in London's Marylebone Road. Historically the scariest waxworks weren't the ones in her museum, but the funny little images in wax that witches made to maim and kill their enemies.

Witches made a little model of wax or clay that resembled their intended victim. (Sometimes these models would be made of the 'earth' of a dead man.) Then they attached a bit of cloth or hair that belonged to the victim to the model. Sometimes the model was baptised, then pins would be stuck into the model. Or sometimes it was burned or buried.

The victim would feel awful stabbing pains, as if dreadful red-hot pokers had been driven into them. Sometimes they would even waste away – they had been bewitched to death.

Weird waxworks have been around for aeons. In the tenth century a woman was drowned at London Bridge for making an image of a bloke called Alessi and pricking it with nails.

In 1538 there was a terrific fuss about a wax baby which was discovered with two pins stuck in it. The baby was about to be buried in a London churchyard.

The gossips claimed it was fashioned by enemies of the Tudor Prince Edward, the younger brother of Princess Elizabeth. It was claimed that the young prince would waste away as the wax was eaten up by worms and decay. A writer named Poole, who was a great wizard, was called in and he said the person who made it was a hopeless witch who didn't know their magical ABC. Poole said the waxwork should have been buried in horse dung if the charm was to work.

The waxwork dolly didn't seem to kill Prince Edward but the unlucky boy died young anyway.

Queen Elizabeth I was attacked by image magic too. In 1578 three wax figures were found buried in the stables of an Islington wizard. The main figure was dressed like Queen Bess and had the word Elizabeth written across the forehead. The other two were dressed like her counsellors. All the figures were covered with magical signs and stuck through with pigs' bristles. As we know, they didn't work and Elizabeth lived on for another twenty-five years.

But she was lucky, because waxworks could be DEADLY.

Ferdinando, Earl of Derby, was a familiar figure at Queen Liz's court. He was called the Wizard Earl, because he hung out with warlocks and sorcerers like John Dee and Sir Walter Raleigh. In 1594 he died suddenly. When his bedroom was searched a wax image was found with hair like the earl's 'twisted through the belly'. Most people blamed the dolly for the earl's death.

Closer to home spells are still cast and models are made. *The New York Times* of 14 December 1900 reported the burning of a pin-studded doll outside the American embassy in London.

In the middle of the last century one London woman made a waxwork of the lady who had run off with her husband and cast it into the fire chanting, 'Burn, you white witch, burn!' The cursed husband-stealer got a terrific headache and fell very sick before the cause of the supernatural enchantment was discovered.

CHAPTER TWO

Cats, Bats, Rats and Other Nasty Pets

THE BROOMSTICK QUARTERLY

Wapping, 15 March 1602

CLASSIFIED RECRUITMENT SECTION

Hear ye animals large and small
Come in your hordes at our witching call
We want cats, bats, frogs and mice
Dogs and rabbits, toads and lice

We'll suckle you on our witches' blood
Use you to cause thunder and flood
You'll be busy playing the unholy fool
And we'll keep you warm in a pot of wool

The pay is all the damned could desire
You'll wreak all the mischief to which you aspire
The hours are really bloody good
And you'll never want for drink or food

If interested in post pls apply to Old Mother Samson,
42 Crooked Lane, London E19
(Send application by owl)
PS Do-gooders, guides and fluffy animals need not apply.
PPS If you pass the test I'll give you a funny name like
Pyewacket, Grizel Greedigut, Tyffin, Tyttey, Lightfoot,
Jezebell or Vinegar Tom
(These are genuine historical witch names.)

The one accessory the full-blooded English witch had to have was not a broomstick or a cauldron but a familiar. A familiar was a sort of witch's pet; it could be a cat, a dog, a frog, a mouse or even a snail, fly or tiny creepy-crawly.

The wizard John Bysack (who was put to death by Witchfinder General Mathew Hopkins during his reign of terror in 1645–46) confessed to having six snails as familiars. He loved them so much he gave them nicknames. He said, 'Each snail was an assassin with a particular mission. Atleward killed cows, Jeffry pigs, Peter sheep, Pyman fowls, Sacar horses and Sydiake Christians.'

These familiars were the witches' personal hotline to the Devil. They would take messages to and fro. When the witch wanted a piece of badness done, her little imp would sneak into the night and do its worst.

In return the witch would give the familiar food, shelter – often in a little pot filled with wool or straw – and company. Witches adored their familiars and familiars loved their witches in return. In fact the sceptical – though there weren't many of them around in those smelly days – said that

22

familiars were really often just pets and that witches were mostly lonely old women who loved their pets.

Like a mother suckling a baby, witches were meant to feed their familiars with their own blood. Any mole or wart or funny bit sticking out from the skin could be used as evidence that the witch had an extra teat – which their familiar would feed on like a little demon sproglet.

It sounds too silly to be true. But don't snigger too fast. In the darkest times of our history a little wart could be enough to get you hanged for witchcraft!

Elizabeth Sawyer, a witch who lived in Edmonton, North London, gave a very full account of how she met her familiar in 1621:

It is eight years since our first acquaintance and three times in the week the devil would come and see me, he would come sometimes in the morning and sometimes in the evening. Always in the shape of a dog, sometimes black and sometimes white. He asked permission to suck my blood and I let him. When he came barking that he had done the mischief I asked I would call him Tom and he would wag his tail.

Some witches and wizards were believed not only to keep animals as familiars but to be able to turn themselves into them at will. Witches usually transformed into hares and cats while wizards became dogs and wolves – particularly hairy wizards who could become werewolves.

How to Transform Yourself into a Beastie

Buy a witch's robe and black hat. Paint silver stars on your ceiling. Cultivate a few moles and a friendship with a stray cat (preferably black). Then follow the advice of witch Isobel Gowdie, who in 1662 revealed the lines she would recite three times to turn herself into a hare:

I shall go into a hare
With Sorrow and sighing and mickle* care
And I shall go in the Devil's name
Till I come home again.
(*much)

To change herself back into a human she would say these words three times:

Hare, Hare, God send thee care.
I am in a Hare's likeness now
But I shall be in a woman's likeness even now.

Isobel could also transform herself into a cat by replacing hare for cat! Black cats got such a spooky reputation that they were actually believed to be the Devil in human form – in the Middle Ages black cats were hunted and killed on Shrove Tuesday and Easter Day.

The toad was another animal that got a nasty reputation. People thought that the warty horns on a toad's head were just like the Devil's. In 1582 Ales Hunt, who lived outside London in St Osyth, Essex, confessed she had two imps and that her sister Margerie Sammon had two toads, one called Tom and the other called Robbyn. Apparently their old ma, Mother Barnes, gave the two sisters their sprites.

Toads were very useful in spell casting as well as being ace familiars. Modern scientists have discovered that witches were onto something. When they are injured toads give off a poisonous substance, called bufagin, or toad's milk. Witches used toad's milk for all sorts of nasty magic spells. Toad's poo was used in flying potions and a lotion of sow-thistle sap and toad's spittle could make the witch invisible.

The witches in William Shakespeare's *Macbeth* knew all about the importance of toads (so much so that they get pride of place in the cauldron!):

> **Round about the cauldron go;**
> **In the poison'd entrails throw;**
> **Toad, that under cold stone ...**
> **[Has] Swelt'red venom ...**
> **Boil thou first i'th' charmed pot**

The stones toads had in their foreheads could also protect the wearer against bad luck. Some rings set with toads' stones have been found from the Middle Ages.

A familiar was often passed down from mother to daughter – talk about a rotten legacy! – or was a present from a witch. Agnes Waterhouse of Hatfield, Essex confessed in 1566 that she had a white spotted cat, which she turned into a toad. This animal was given to her by Elisabeth Francis. She used the cat to kill cows and finally to knock off her husband as well as a neighbour and his wife who had got on her nerves.

But this was a cat with a past. Elisabeth Francis had received it from her own grandma and sweet Liz used it first to kill her own baby – who annoyed her perhaps by bawling too much – and then to lame her husband.

26

But familiars were fickle creatures. Most seemed to have not been seen for dust when their mistress or master was in deep trouble.

From menacing sheep, startling babies and blinding the neighbours, the naughty imps – in most cases – vanished off the face of the earth when their witch employers were arrested.

That's gratitude for you.

CHAPTER THREE

Witches in the Palace

Lots of witches and wizards were poor old crones and cronies who lived on mouldy bread and faggots and worked their deadly magic in the middle of the backwoods miles from the bright city lights.

But in London another fancier type of sorcerer flourished. And lords and ladies, kings and queens weren't above trying to use a little magic to stick a lance or sword into their enemies – or improve their own chances of fame and fortune.

But it was dangerous to meddle in royal circles. Or to merely predict how long a ruler would live. For example, in 1213 Peter the Wise, a Yorkshire magician, was hanged for (correctly) foretelling the tragic end to King John's reign.

The King's Pigeon

Brandon was a royal wizard attached to King Henry VIII's court. One day, walking in the courtyard with a bunch of nobles and hangers-on, Brandon pointed to a pigeon sitting on top of the wall.

28

'I'll bet I can kill that bird stone dead without touching it,' he told the disbelieving courtiers.

Taking a piece of chalk, Brandon drew an outline of the bird on the ground. Then he took a knife and plunged it into the heart of the drawing. The bird toppled off the wall – dead as a doorknob.

As you can imagine, people didn't mess with Brandon after that. But King Henry VIII – who was always imagining plots against his rather vast royal person – forbade Brandon from practising any more such magic.

He reasoned that the wizard could as easily top a king as a pigeon.

Sometimes accusations of sorcery were easy ways for kings to deal with people they took a dislike to. In 1419 Henry IV, for example, accused his hated stepmother Joan of Navarre of attempting to murder him by magic. Her chaplain confessed after torture to conjuring and necromancy. (Necromancy means magic or sorcery and sometimes involves calling up the spirits of the dead.)

The king had his stepmother imprisoned in Leeds Castle. But a few days before he died in 1422 he forgave her and allowed her back to London and returned her wealth – maybe because he was tormented by a guilty conscience.

The queen most tarred by witchcraft was Elizabeth Woodville, daughter of a humble knight, who secretly married King Edward IV in 1464. The king's counsellors and other nobles were horrified. Though she was a bit of medieval crumpet (pretty, that is) Elizabeth was no match for the king in wealth and poshness. The rumour that she bewitched him swept the land.

The king's brother, the jealous Duke of Clarence, went even further and accused Edward himself of using necromancy by burning an enchanted candle to destroy him.

In May 1477 two close friends of the Duke of Clarence, Thomas Burdett and John Stacy, were executed for plotting to destroy the king and prince of Wales by wax images of them – then burning them. Stacy was a well-known wizard and he confessed to necromancy.

But the Duke of Clarence was mightily annoyed. He burst

into the royal council chamber and defended his friends while (foolishly) publicly accusing the king and queen of sorcery.

The king had his brother sent to the Tower of London, where a few months later he mysteriously perished. According to legend he was drowned in a butt of malmsey – a barrel of beer.

Edward certainly had a run of rotten brothers. His other brother, who eventually became Richard III, spent a lot of his time plotting to seize the throne, from Edward's son, his own nephew. It's believed – though never finally proven – that after Edward's death in 1483 Richard had his nephews, the young princes, murdered in the Tower of London.

When Richard III came to power he revived the rumours that Queen Elizabeth was a witch in an effort to prove that her son (and, of course, his brother Edward IV's son), Edward V, was not the legal heir to the throne.

One day in the council chamber, he suddenly piped up and asked the assembled lords what punishment those traitors who conspired against his life should receive. When he was assured they should be punished, Richard shook his withered left arm before the horrified nobles and told them that the evil magic of the ex-queen and the former mistress

31

of Edward IV – Jane Shore – had together done this to him. (According one witness all the nobles realized that Richard had been born with a withered arm but were too scared to point this out.)

The powerful Lord Hastings, who had timidly tried to protect the queen and the former king's mistress was arrested and executed immediately without trial. And Jane Shore – whom snobby Richard hated because she was the commoner daughter of a cloth merchant – was forced to walk the streets of London naked, except for a skimpy dress called a kirtle, and carrying a candle.

But Richard's plan backfired. The public didn't believe Jane was a witch and her modesty and grace enchanted the crowds. She was sent to prison in London where the king's solicitor Thomas Lynom fell in love with her and wanted to marry her. (She may not have been a witch but she certainly was bewitching!)

Meanwhile the ex-queen was safe in sanctuary in Westminster Palace. But soon Richard had an act passed that her marriage had been the result of 'sorcery and witchcraft committed by the said Elizabeth and her mother Jaquetta, Duchess of Bedford.'

This act put it in writing (if not in truth) that King Richard was the real and proper king after all.

Bewitching Boleyn

Henry VIII's six wives were, on the whole, not much luckier than Richard III's victims. Their fate is well summed up by the rhyme: 'Divorced, beheaded, died. Divorced, beheaded, survived.'

Once his wife-killing habits were known, the heart of many a Tudor lass must have sunk when the roving eye of pudgy Henry settled on her. But Anne Boleyn (c.1504–1536), Henry's second wife, was a smart lady who coveted the power that being queen would give her.

She married Henry secretly in 1533, six years after their affair began – and before he was properly divorced from his wife Catherine of Aragon. Henry split from the Catholic Church and founded the new Church of England because they wouldn't let him divorce Catherine and wed Anne.

But once their relationship was public he lost interest in Anne. Vitally she couldn't give him a male heir (despite producing England's greatest queen).

Henry accused Anne of being a witch. But what evidence was held to damn her?

A) She had a tiny extra finger on her hand

B) She had a big mole on her neck

C) Henry caught her riding through the air on a broomstick

D) She had lots of miscarriages

E) She had a third nipple

F) She was caught with a white hare in her bed

Answer: All of the above except C and F. According to many accounts Anne did have a third nipple - though others say she didn't.

Anne was also accused of affairs with her own brother and four commoners. Blatant inaccuracies in the times she was meant to have had her affairs were ignored because a witch could ride through space on her broomstick. On 19 May 1536 she was beheaded at the Tower of London. Her ghost is said to ride in her final resting place – the Chapel of St Peter ad Vinculam in the Tower – on every 19 May.

Queen Elizabeth and her Sorcerers Soft Spot

Perhaps because of her mother's unhappy life and reputation for witchcraft Queen Elizabeth was quite soft on sorcerers. We will learn later how she took the famous wizard John Dee under her wing.

However her counsellors were quite paranoid that sorcery was being used against her life. Little wonder when wild Catholic plots to put her arch rival Mary, Queen of Scots on the throne flourished. Supernatural plots were especially feared – much more so than ordinary poisonings and stabbings.

One of the most serious plots was discovered in 1562 when Arthur and Edmund Pole and Anthony Fortescue were charged with trying to oust Liz and place Mary on the throne. Professional wizard John Prestall had been employed by the Poles to invoke evil spirits. They were charged with finding out from these demons how to kill the queen.

Prestall was a well-known wizard. Strangely Elizabeth treated him very gently. He was sent to the Tower but released five years later when he offered to turn silver into gold. In 1571 he was again charged with magical plotting against Elizabeth and was sentenced to death. But Liz reduced his punishment to life imprisonment. Somehow he got out of the Tower and was heard of twenty years later still practising wizardry.

King James All at Sea

If you want to cause a storm at sea and sink the ship of an enemy, do you?

A) Make a wax model of a ship and drown it in a bucket of water

B) Dress up as a mermaid and go swimming in the local pool while chanting magic incantations

C) Throw an enchanted cat into the sea

D) Charter a speedboat and crash it in the path of the enemy's ship?

ANSWER: c) This method was tried by Dr Fian, a notorious
Scottish wizard and schoolmaster. He wanted to kill
Scotland's King James VI (the future King James I of
England) who was on his way to Denmark to visit his bride
Princess Anne. King James's ship was nearly wrecked in the
storm but he was saved because, James himself claimed, he
was a man of God. Fian and his accomplices were horribly
tortured when they were caught in 1591.

Fian had his feet crushed in a horrible pair of iron shoes
that got smaller and smaller, called 'the bootes'. King James
'took great delight' to watch, according to one
contemporary, while all his fingernails were pulled out with a
pair of pincers and needles inserted under what was left of
them. Then Fian was strangled and finally burnt.

King James was convinced of the truth of the sorcery
when one of the accused, Agnes Sampson, told him the
actual words spoken between him and Princess Anne on their
wedding night.

As a result of this brush with magic, King James got really
obsessed with witches and plots against his royal person.
After seven years of research, in 1597, he published a book
all about their wicked arts called the *Daemonologie*. In this
book he argued that all witches, except children, should be
sentenced to death. When he became king of England in

1603 he passed a tough new law punishing witchcraft by death. Till then only people accused of using witchcraft to cause murder were executed.

Some historians say many nasty witch persecutions in England were set off by the witch-hater James. But others point out that actually he was quite fair-minded. In his later years especially he began to fancy himself as a bit of a detective and intervened several times to save people unfairly accused of witchcraft.

In one case a woman had horrible fits when she heard the first verse of St John's Gospel. The woman claimed to have been enchanted by an evil witch so that she couldn't bear to hear the words from the Bible. But the woman was shamming, she failed to recognize the same verse from St John's Gospel in Greek. In another Leicester case the Sleuth King detected that a young boy – who had already accused nine women and seen them swing from the gibbet (i.e. seen them hang) – was a fantastic fibber. The king probably saved the life of another six women who were under arrest.

In fact the king saw so many shams and frauds that according to a Church historian of the time 'he began flatly to deny the working of witches and devils as falsehoods and delusions.'

It is ironic then that the king who started by seeing witches everywhere ended up believing that he had found them practically nowhere!

LONDON WITCH WATCH

Name: Anne Bodenham

Imp: A little toad she wore in a bag around her neck

Witchery: Anne Bodenham was a servant to the notorious Dr Lambe, who was killed by a London mob for being a wizard in 1640. His servant Anne was always under suspicion. She'd learnt a great deal about herbs and potions, drawing magic circles and charms. Thirteen years after Dr Lambe's death, she was accused by a servant girl, Annie Styles, of drawing a magic circle and conjuring Beelzebub, Tormentor, Lucifer and Satan. Styles also claimed Anne turned herself into a big black cat and had made her buy poisons to kill her employer.

Verdict: Bodenham was executed in 1653, despite bravely protesting her innocence and despite Styles breaking down and going back on her accusations.

CHAPTER FOUR

Mirror, Mirror

You can see into the future. You know when old Mrs Waterbottle-Tibbs's cat will die and you can predict whether Man U will win the FA Cup. Your gift comes in dead useful. No one can beat you at cards. And sometimes you can help people avoid disaster.

But ...

You can see illness and death. You can't move without seeing pain and suffering. The more you see the more you ask, 'Is my gift really a curse?'

The ability to see into the future was a mark of many (though not all) of the great London witches and wizards.

Simon Forman – who was a great wizard – successfully predicted his own death in the very week it took place. One can just picture the scene. One sunny summer day, over the morning *Wizard Gazette* and scrambled eggs, old Simon had a word with his wife:

'Oh, by the way dear, I'm going to kick the bucket later this week. Hope you don't mind.'

History doesn't record Mrs Forman's reaction, but in the event Simon keeled over while crossing the River Thames in a boat.

Dr Forman was half-quack doctor and half-sorcerer. The courts and the proper doctors held him in scorn.

But to Londoners he was a hero. This was because he did what most of the posh clerics and doctors didn't do. He stayed in London along with the mass of poor people when bubonic plague gripped the capital in 1592 and 1594. He cured himself as well as many patients with his potions. (The plague was a putrid illness. It causes victims to grow giant sores called buboes, which turned blackish purple. Sufferers would die in screaming agony.) Given that no one – absolutely no one – at the time knew what caused the plague or had managed to cure it – this was life and death magic. Forman was so proud of his achievement he made up a poem about it:

> **And in the time of pestilent plague**
> **When doctors all did fly**
> **And got them into places far**
> **From out the city**
> **The Lord appointed me to stay**
> **To cure the sick and sore**
> **But not the rich and mighty ones**
> **But the distressed poor.**

After his death, however, Forman's reputation got a real blow when he was implicated in bloody murder.

Forman had got entangled with a vengeful woman, the Countess of Essex. To begin with he gave her potions to make her then husband, the Earl of Essex, ill. The countess was able to get a divorce from her husband and set out to catch the Earl of Somerset. Apparently Forman helped her win his love by making wax dollies.

The Countess and Earl of Somerset were married in 1613 but Forman was already dead. However he had left her a parting gift in the form of an introduction to the witch Mrs Anne Turner.

The plot thickened when the Earl of Somerset's friend Sir Thomas Overbury tried to warn him of the nefarious magic that his wife was so fond of using. Soon Overbury was dead – poisoned!

Mrs Turner was charged with murdering Overbury to please the countess. The poor Earl of Somerset was also implicated in the murder and Simon Forman's reputation was dragged through the mud. King James I pardoned the toffs (the count and earl) but Mrs Turner was hanged at Tyburn as a murderess!

Forman had the gift of prophecy. But other sorcerers – like the great Elizabethan scholar Dr John Dee – just didn't have it or the related gift of 'skrying' or seeing spirits.

In many cases children were discovered to be skryers. Some wizards believed this was because children had not become used to looking at things in an un-seeing adult way. They were still in touch with their 'inner eye'.

Magicians tended their skills by looking in magic mirrors and crystal balls and sometimes – when their 'inner eye' absolutely refused to see – by employing 'skryers'.

Fried Eggs for the Wizard

The sorcerer's den is brimming with mystery. On the walls hang drawings of pentacles and triangles and weird symbols of another language. In the middle there is a mirror, but one so strange that most people are scared to look in it. And on the table, covered with a cloth of purple velvet, is a crystal ball.

The den is festooned with cobwebs and dust because no one is brave enough to come in to do the cleaning – and the sorcerer can't be bothered with mops and dusters.

Gazing into the crystal ball the 'skryer' can see visions of angels and devils of crimes that have been committed and those that are still to come. Thieves have been caught red-handed by his visions.

But a real skryer can see in many things – not just mirrors and crystals. Any shiny surface – a fingernail anointed with magic potion, the glittering blade of a sword, a beryl stone, a bowl of perfectly still water – can reveal strange secrets.

In the Orient mirrors made of Indian ink were used to tell the future. In London a similar feat was achieved by putting the white of a newly laid egg under a beer glass and exposing it to the hot summer sun.

So remember, if you have the gift, there is more than one use for a fried egg!

It's a bad idea to rub a skryer up the wrong way, they know too many things. The preacher John Wesley wrote in 1761 in his diary how a young lad had seen the very act of a murder in the crystal belonging to a famous warlock. Just imagine it. The cloudy ball, the knife blade stabbing in and out, the crimson blood – and the boy bewildered by what he had seen.

Often, in fact, ordinary folk were better skryers than trained sorcerers. In 1476 Nazareth Jarbrey visited the London magician Thomas Barley in his house in Totell Street, Westminster. Jarbrey looked into a beryl stone belonging to the magician and saw the man who stole a casket of pearls and jewels belonging to his mother.

Soon Jarbrey was able to give up his day job – he was so good at skrying that even vicars came to him for help.

The Tragic Case of Dr Dee

One of the most famous sorcerers in London's history was Dr John Dee and he was protected by the great Queen Elizabeth I herself.

John Dee, born in London in 1527, was a very clever man who was way ahead of many of his rather dull contemporaries. As a Cambridge student he had staged a Greek comedy in which, by means of pulleys and ropes, he made one of his actors fly about the stage on the back of a large scarab. But many in his audience – which included posh lords and ladies – were so convinced that they had seen a man flying that they fainted. From this people were convinced that Dee the brilliant scholar was really a weird wizard.

In 1555 Dee had an unlucky brush with the Law when he was accused along with three others of plotting the death of Queen Mary by magic and of calculating the lifespan of Princess Elizabeth – the next in line to the throne. One of the accusers, John Ferrys, claimed that as soon as he charged Dee with black magic one of his children died and the other was blinded.

Dee was tried by the Star Chamber and was thankfully acquitted. Historians think that what actually happened was that he was asked to cast a horoscope of Princess Elizabeth

– which was a very risky thing to do given that Queen Mary was paranoid about her young rival to the throne.

Dee continued his studies abroad and his fame grew. When Queen Liz came to the throne in 1558 she asked him to fix by star-gazing a lucky date for her coronation by star-gazing. He became a firm favourite of the Virgin Queen – she was even said to have become his pupil after the publication of one of his books. Alas for Dee she never gave him a job with a decent bit of money so he always had to scrape around for dosh.

Like Dr Forman, Dee was obsessed with the Philosopher's Stone. Unlike Forman he did not have the gift of seeing the future or seeing spirits in crystal so he got a series of skryers to help him out. Inevitably sometimes they were more rascals than seers.

The biggest rogue – though he was a man with strange skrying gifts – was called Edward Kelly.

Kelly was decidedly dodgy. As a young man he had had his ears cut off for forgery and he always wore a black skull cap to conceal his missing lobes. Before he met Dee he had been engaged in digging up dead bodies and raising spirits in the dead of night in graveyards.

Dee adored Kelly and listened entranced as Kelly saw spirits in Dee's magic ball or speculum. This is what Dee might have written to his wife about Kelly:

Dear Jane,

Ed is a great bloke – much better than all the other rotten so-called skryers I have put up with. He is a blessing to me from heaven and has a marvellous gift of seeing spirits. The other day he saw an angel called Uriel. Uriel has given Ed some great news: there are forty-nine good 'spirits of light' who will come and speak to us in the magic crystal.

Another angel, Madimi, has also visited. She is seven or eight and the most delightful and naughty urchin that you can imagine. She has long hair rolled up on her head and hanging down behind her. And she wears a green dress which has a beautiful train.

Madimi ran and hopped all over my books. I asked her, 'Whose maiden are you?' and she replied, the naughty sprite, 'Whose man are you?'

She told me as well that she was the last but one of her mother's children and that she could not tell me where she lived, else she would be beaten.

But, my dear Jane, I have grave news. The spirits have told Kelly that we must quit our dear home in Mortlake and go with Count Albert Laski, Prince of Siradia, to Poland. Kelly says the angels have predicted great things for the Count, he is to be King of Poland, and we have a sacred calling to help him.

I know you'll be sad, dear Jane, to leave your pretty house and family. But we creatures of the spirit must follow a higher calling.

Your loving

Johnny

So Dee and Kelly, with their wives in tow, set off for Poland with Count Laski, whom Dee had met at Queen Liz's court. As Dee left a mob – who believed him to be an evil wizard – stormed his house at Mortlake, went right through his priceless collection of books and manuscripts and destroyed many of his instruments.

Dee and Kelly didn't do as well as they had hoped on the continent. Laski turned out to be far poorer than they thought and after a while, particularly when their experiments with gold and alchemy became too expensive, they had to leave him. They became wandering magicians, little better than beggars when their luck was out.

Sometimes they found favour at court, such as the bigwig Emperor Rudolph II of Prague. Meanwhile Kelly was becoming more and more obsessed with the secret of the Philosopher's Stone and less and less interested in crystal balls, which as it didn't involve loadsa money, seemed to him a waste of time.

Then hey presto, Kelly did it. He found the closely guarded secret of the Philosopher's Stone. His sister and Dee's son claim they saw him making gold. At the time he was living as guest of the wealthy Count Rosenberg in Bohemia. He suddenly became very wealthy and popular and was knighted as Sir Ed Kelly (surprise, surprise).

Now, Kelly probably didn't tell Dee how it was done. But it was certain that Kelly had quite a hold on him. And then to top it all, Kelly, who had always fancied Dee's wife, now told him that the angels had commanded him that they must share their wives.

Well, Dee wasn't terribly keen on sharing his wife Jane – who was very pretty – and she was even less keen. But he agreed, as it was what God had commanded, according to the know-all Kelly.

But it was the beginning of the end. Soon Dee and Jane had got tired of the whole thing and the foursome began to quarrel. Six years after he had left Dee sailed back to England. Soon he had an audience with the Queen herself, who wanted the secret of turning iron into gold for England.

But the magical powers had deserted Dee. He complained that his magical instruments in his house at Mortlake had been destroyed. Though Queen Liz lost faith in his powers she didn't abandon him. But after her death he was increasingly poverty-stricken and forgotten. (The next ruler, King James I, was far too suspicious of witches and sorcerers to look after Dee.)

Dee died in Mortlake in 1604, a poor old man. But his memory and his reams of writings about spirits and magic have survived. As have his speculum and magic mirror which can be seen in the British Museum.

And what of Kelly, you say? Perhaps he got his just desserts. Emperor Rudy got a bit possessive about the Philosopher's Stone and all it could do, and was keeping Kelly a virtual prisoner. One night in 1593 Kelly tried to escape but fell off a wall and badly injured himself, eventually dying from his wounds. And, yes, you could be forgiven for saying, Why didn't he see that coming?

CHAPTER FIVE

Hubble Bubble, Spells and Potions

The spells in this chapter are genuine witches' spells. But don't try them at home – you've got to be a real witch to make them work properly. You have been warned!

To Cure Warts

Stroke the wart with a snail and then stick a thorn through the snail (this is not for the tender hearted or the squeamish).

The Truly Terrible Black Fast

Don't eat any meat or milk or food made with milk.
Meanwhile concentrate all your witchly powers on your
victim till he or she dies. This horrible fast can also be used
to make a thief return stolen goods. In 1538 Mabel Briggs
was accused of fasting for the death of King Henry VIII as
well as the Duke of Norfolk. Nobody believed her defence
that she was only using it to get some stolen things back.
The king and duke were in fact unharmed by
Mabel's fast, so maybe she was innocent.
But soon after his death, wild rumours
swept the land that the king had in fact
died from black magic.

To Cure Burns

Breathe three times on the burnt place and say
these words:

Here come I to cure a burnt sore
If the dead know what the living endure
The burnt sore would burn no more

This charm was used by an East London wizard, who his
patients said always cured them and no scar showed
afterwards, however horrid the original burn.

To Make a Friend or Relative Rich Quick

No, not the national lottery – your chances are pretty slim there...

Find a good broomstick with stout twigs in it and rake all the dirt of your town or village towards the door of the person you want to make rich while chanting your own version of this charm:

> **To the house of William, my son**
> **Hie all the dirt of Kilkenny town**

This was the charm practised by Dame Alice Kytler of Kilkenny Ireland in 1324. Her husband Sir John Le Poer thought she had made away with two previous husbands and suspected she was up to the same

tricks with him. Townspeople claimed that she was trying to get money for her adored son William Outlaw and heard her chanting the above verse. There is no reason why the verse shouldn't work in London. If you live in Clapham for example you could try

To the house of Katie, my sister
Hie all the wealth of Clapham town

(Let's hope Katie is grateful for your efforts.)

A Witch's Love Cake

A witch has to get sweaty and then clean off the sweat with flour. This flour should be mixed with bits of her burnt hair, some oil and an egg or two . Then the cake is fed to the man the witch is in love with. The victim is said to fall violently in love with the witch. But if you can get someone to eat this yuck-sounding cake you must be a pretty good witch anyway!

Another Love Potion

Draw some blood from your veins, dry it and then make it into a fine powder. Mix your powdered blood with equal portions of ground heart of dove, liver of sparrow, womb of swallow and kidney of hare. Give

the potion to the man or woman you want to fall in love with you. But, again, how do you make them drink the potion? Answers on the back of a postcard, please.

Two Flying Potions

1. Mix parsley, water of aconite, poplar leaves and soot.

2. Mix parsnip, sweet flag, cinquefoil, bat's blood, deadly nightshade and oil.

These things are actual historical ingredients of witches' flying potions. According to one historian they showed that witches were pretty good at their poisons – deadly nightshade and aconite are two of the most deadly plants that grow in Europe. Witches might actually have been early drug addicts – instead of flying when they smeared these potions on themselves and their broomsticks they might have suffered from very powerful hallucinations. On the other hand, who are we to tell – maybe they DID fly.

The first potion is watery and would not cause delusions. But the second is an ointment which could cause excitement and weird visions.

Be warned! It is better to leave these things to trained wizards – DON'T EXPERIMENT. These are deadly, horrible poisons that can cause fits and death if they come into contact with your skin.

Other flying potions contained atropine. Some witch historians believe that people who rubbed atropine on their skin might have suffered from very powerful hallucinations of flying. Atropine is now used, very carefully, by doctors for treating fits.

CHAPTER SIX

Witchfinders

The witch craze was a horrid blood sport that took hold of Europe. The whole place, stuck in a mouldy morass of bogs, foul food and disgusting diseases like the plague went loony. Europe became a hellhole of smoke and burning witch pyres.

Men had to have someone to blame – and often they took out their anger on the nearest thing to hand – their wives, mums and daughters. Almost any woman became a witch suspect. In fact in some places a definition of a witch was practically a two-legged creature in a skirt!

Here in London we were a little bit more restrained than the Germans or the Scots, for example, who were two of the worst offenders. We didn't tend to inflict hideous tortures on suspected witches – with just the odd wizard thrown in – till crushed, bleeding and mutilated they confessed to almost anything.

But though we weren't as nasty as some of our neighbours, we shouldn't pat ourselves on the back too soon. There was one man who created a huge mountain of corpses almost single-handedly.

That man was Mathew Hopkins, the son of a clergyman from Manningtree in Essex. Failing to make a go of it as a lawyer, Hopkins took up an even more cut-throat career – as the self-proclaimed Witchfinder General. Hopkins spread fear and terror wherever he went, which he seems to have enjoyed. And he also made a lot of dosh from the locals who would load him down with gold for detecting witches.

It is estimated that between 1644 and 1646 Hopkins and his assistant John Stearne raked in between £300 and £1000 – not bad going when the average wage was sixpence a day!

Hopkins had three hundred to four hundred witches killed – more than all the other English witch-hunters put together.

Hopkins' bloody career took off in his own home town of Manningtree. He claimed witches used to hold meetings near his house. During one of these get-togethers Hopkins – who just happened to be hanging around nearby – overheard a witch ask her imp to find a certain Elizabeth Clarke.

Conveniently for Hopkins, Clarke just happened to be a poor, one-legged, defenceless old woman. It would have been another matter if she'd been rich or noble. But nobody cared how much you bullied a poverty-stricken old dame.

Clarke was taken into custody and kept awake for three days and nights. On the fourth night, exhausted and weeping, she told Hopkins that if he stayed she would call her imps. Hey presto, a cat, a white dog and a greyhound called Vinegar Tom appeared. Soon poor old Clarke was naming names with a vengeance. At least twenty-three and maybe up to thirty-one women were accused of witchcraft.

The evidence against these women wasn't exactly watertight.

One woman was suspected chiefly because a hare was seen outside her house! She admitted she'd seen the hare but quite reasonably denied she was a witch.

Now Hopkins had assistants and a flood of cronies, who maybe partly to stop suspicion pointing to them, mercilessly wrung confessions out of dozens of women.

And so it went on. The confused women outdid each other with their colourful and ridiculous confessions. We know that at least sixteen women – and maybe eleven or twelve more – were put to death.

But for Hopkins his home town Manningtree was just the start of good thing. He continued his witch-hunting, spreading his net to Suffolk and other eastern counties.

As the piles of bodies with broken necks mounted up, the Witchfinder General got quite a system going. For every county he employed four searchers (two men and two women). Hopkins even had a favourite searcher, a woman called Goody Phillips. These were the people who stripped the poor suspected witches and searched them for the Devil's marks.

The clergyman John Gaule knew all the wicked tricks Hopkins used to get confessions. He wrote how after being stripped naked the suspect 'is placed in the middle of the room upon a stool or table, crosse-legged or in some other uneasy posture, to which if she submits not, she is then bound with cords, there she is watched and kept without meat for the space of twenty-four hours.'

The watchers – as we know – were on the look-out for imps and familiars. And as the merest fly could count as a familiar, they nearly always found them. Ludicrous confessions soon followed.

But luckily for hundreds of innocent women Hopkins was getting too big for his boots. A few sane people, including judges and clerics, started asking questions and storm clouds gathered over his head. His more horrible methods – like swimming (see p. 65) – were banned – and he was personally hauled over the coals, accused among other things of fleecing gullible people for his own profit.

Among those who turned against Hopkins was the Reverend John Gaule, who preached against him and hinted that Hopkins himself might be a witch.

His fall was as sudden as his rise. By early 1646 the number of witches Hopkins discovered dried up. Suddenly there didn't seem to be a witch under every hedgerow and every household pet wasn't really an imp plotting the Devil's work.

There are two explanations for Hopkins' death in 1646. Some historians say he died of consumption. Others claim that he was accused of witchcraft and was himself hanged as a witch. Which just goes to show what a dicey profession being a Witchfinder General was.

WAS OLIVER CROMWELL A WIZARD?

Some people say that Hopkins only got away with his evil deeds because the rest of the country was too preoccupied with the Civil War. This was fought between the Roundheads led by the Puritan Oliver Cromwell and the Royalists who supported the then king, foppish King Charles I.

Some people even thought that Oliver Cromwell was a wizard. How else, they reasoned, could a man born in Huntingdon in 1599 as the mere son of a country gent get to a position where by 1653 he was the uncrowned king of England?

The key to Cromwell's success was the battle of Naseby – fought in 1645 – where Cromwell brilliantly commanded the Roundhead troops. This battle really laid waste to King Chas's army and the king himself was captured. But people again whispered that Cromwell used military trickery that amounted to wizardry.

King Charles was executed for treason on 30 January 1649. The gossips said that ghoulish Cromwell went several times to view the dead body. But what all the rumour boiled down to was how could a normal, average, everyday sort of squire become uncrowned king if he wasn't a wizard?

TEN WICKED WAYS OF SPOTTING A WITCH

1. PRICKING

Prick the witch's skin with a sharp needle. If it does not draw blood she is a witch. But some unscrupulous 'prickers', who just wanted their dosh when the witch was hanged, faked the test by using spring-loaded knives with retractable pins! In other cases women who were stripped naked in public were so scared that their blood literally froze. The nasty 'pricker' could then boast he had found another witch and collect his blood money.

2. SWIMMING

Witches were chucked into ponds with their right hand bound to their left toe, and ropes holding them up. The barmy theory was that the pure water of baptism would reject witches. If they floated they were witches – and they often floated because of the weird way they were bound and held up with ropes. If they sank they were innocent, but probably dead. Talk about a loaded test! Swimming was banned in 1646.

3. THE DUCKING STOOL

Women were strapped into a chair and plunged into a nearby pond. They could be ducked for a whole day. Sometimes this punishment was also used against minor criminals or women who nagged their husbands! It was always horrid and often fatal.

4. THE WITCH'S CRADLE

The accused were tied in sacks and rocked like babies in a cradle. The rocking caused delusions and produced some zany 'confessions'.

5. POTIONS

Hideous potions, sometimes containing mandrake or atropine, were forced on witches or wizards who refused to confess. Under these mind-altering drugs they would 'confess' bizarre details that would delight the witch-hunters.

6. SCALES OF JUSTICE

Giant balance scales were only sometimes used. The witch would be weighed against a giant Bible or some weights. If they were heavier or lighter they would be condemned. Only a perfect balance would make them innocent. Talk about weighting the scales of justice!

7. THE SCOLD'S BRIDLE

A metal cage with a built-in gag that fitted in the mouth. Sometimes the gag had a cruel metal spike which pierced the tongue. This horrible bridle, which was only used on women, came from Scotland and made its appearance around London in the seventeenth century. Sometimes houses had a hook by the fireplace so that when the husband got fed up with his wife he could send for the town jailer to have her bridled and chained to the hook!

8. WITCH MARKS

Any spots or warts or moles could be seen as witch marks – the third teat by which the witch let her familiar suck her blood. Accused women were publicly stripped and searched for marks.

9. WATCHING

The more hideous tortures practised on the continent were banned in England. But witch-hunters often kept the accused awake for days and nights on end while they watched them for familiars. Sleep deprivation is now recognized as gruesome torture. Sometimes they were made to walk around till their feet bled. They would be watched for any familiars to contact them – if a rat made an appearance it would be taken as proof to convict the witch. Not that the prison was vermin-infested.

10. BURNING

Joan of Arc was the most famous woman to be accused of witchcraft and burnt at the stake – by us friendly Brits. In England witches were rarely burnt, and only if they were found guilty of murder. Under the witchcraft act of 1563 death by hanging was only used for those who had used sorcery to murder.

LONDON WITCH WATCH

Name: Joan Butts

Witchery: In 1682 Joan Butts was accused of bewitching a child into having fits. But Joan didn't help herself. She all but admitted it, saying, 'If I have not bewitched the child, if all the devils in Hell could help me, I would bewitch it.' But she claimed she was just mad (as hell) when she cursed the kid. She had a rotten temper: during the trial she turned on one of the witnesses and accused him of selling himself to the Devil!

Verdict: Amazingly Joan was let off by the jury in Southwark, South London. ('It's amazingly difficult to prove someone is a witch,' one bystander was heard to exclaim.)

CHAPTER SEVEN

Hex the Hag – Or How to Protect Yourself from Witchery

In the twenty-first century we have insurance to protect us from menaces like burglars and fires and our homes falling down.

But in the super-spooky witching times how would you protect yourself from the evil all about you?

You couldn't simply walk into your local Abbey National and say, 'I'd like an insurance policy please to protect me against witchcraft with special clauses against magical fits, headaches, murder and my toes dropping off.'

So instead people relied on charms, herbs, gems and special anti-magical devices.

Some of them were really smelly! Garlic hung about your neck or around your house was good for scaring away vampires as well as witches.

And old wee had its uses (apart from storing it up to use as a stinky homemade bleach). You could mix it with wheat and other stuff to make a cake which you burned to break a witch's spell. Or you could put bits of your own hair in a cup of urine, boil it up into a super-pongy brew and throw it on the fire to get rid of a magical headache.

Protect Me from Evil

A nasty witch has hexed you and your family. Your animals are dying and your home is invaded by a foul stench (and, no, it doesn't come from your medieval loo in the middle of your sitting room). To break the witch's curse, do you?

1. Hang some mistletoe in the entrance to your home and kiss all your family underneath it

2. Make a necklace with a cat's-eye gemstone in the middle and wear it at all times

3. Collect your old poo and store it in a tub in front of your house – the smell will put the witch off

4. Make an amulet of salt and herbs and wear it around your neck

5. Mummify your family cat and bury it in your walls in the hope that it will scare away the witch's familiars

6. Put a broomstick across your threshold – the witch will not be able to pass?

ANSWER: All of the above except 3. Lots of herbs, including lavender, St John's Wort and holly were meant to scare away witches. Gems like rubies and amber – as well as salt – were meant to protect you from evil. Dried-out moggies have been discovered in some houses in the south east of England – buried in a position to look like they are still hunting down supernatural vermin. (Cats could work for good Christians as well as witches.) Finally witches were not believed to be able to pass a broomstick on the threshold of a blessed house.

71

You could use broomsticks and dead cats for everyday witchcraft. But what do you do if you want to kill the witch who has put a curse on you?

The answer is obvious. Make a witch bottle!

About 200 witch bottles have been found all over England buried deep in the ground underneath old houses. One was dug up recently in Reigate, Surrey, south of London, buried in a ruined house. Who knows, if you live in an old house and do a bit of digging underneath the fireplace, what you might discover? But it might be an idea to ask your parents first.

Any old wine bottle or oil jar will serve as a witch bottle. Traditionally people used fat clay bottles, decorated with a picture of a grim pot-bellied old geezer, called bellarmines. You can see a bellarmine in the Tower of London where Elizabethan explorer Sir Walter Raleigh was locked up.

Fill the bottle with things that will curse the witch. These could be bent pins, bits of your hair, eyelashes, nails, bones, thorns and pieces of fabric cut into the shapes of hearts. The vital ingredient is a popular and smelly one! Yes, you've guessed it – more wee.

Then you bury the witch bottle in a warm place under the hearth. When the witch goes to the loo she will suffer the most awful agonies and be unable to wee. Some people believed that the witch would even turn up on your doorstep screaming with pain. If the bottle is a really good one the witch may even die!

One good thing about witch bottles is that you don't have to know who the witch is. Just keep a good lookout among your nastier neighbours to see if one unexpectedly passes away.

The witch bottles that have been discovered buried under old houses are the ones that didn't actually work. If the witch dies the bottle is meant to explode – scattering its eyelashes, bent pins and urine far and wide!

CHAPTER EIGHT

Nine of the Devil?

Grown-ups, especially those without sprogs of their own, kid themselves that children are little angels.

Children don't kid themselves.

After all, one visit to the playground is all it takes to figure out that the half-pint bully is just as nasty as the pint-sized one.

In the mists of history there have been some truly demonic children. Sometimes they have been witches and wizards themselves. Worse – and more often – they've been the sort of sneak that points fingers. The sort of little kids that get grown-ups hanged as witches and wizards. What we know now as Greater London – what were once little villages outside London – has been plentifully supplied with these children. There was, for example, the Maid of Thames Street, a girl called Mary Glover. In 1603 Mary claimed she had been bewitched by a Mother Jackson . As soon as Mother Jackson went near her she started having terrible fits. Several doctors thought Mary was faking her fits. But poor Mother Jackson was still thrown into Newgate Prison, where she died.

One of the most famous cases of a child and witchery was reported in the newspapers.

THE LONDON POST AND MAIL

SPECIAL EDITION 1599

One of the strangest cases of witchcraft and possession ever to come before the courts has appeared lately in London before the Bishop of London and Samuel Harsnett, his worthy chaplain.

The case concerns the preacher John Darrel, whose actions have lately caused him to become infamous throughout the land. Darrel is none other than the famous exorcist who has driven demons from several afflicted children.

But are his celebrated exorcisms really the actions of a despicable conman? Londoners have a right to know!

Darrel's latest case concerns an apprentice musician boy by the name of William Somers. This young boy met a suspected witch at a coal pit. He claimed this woman bewitched him. Soon afterwards he began to suffer from fits; laughing like a madman he would find his body twisting and turning into knots. He would foam at the mouth and his belly swelled enormously.

Darrel was called in by concerned citizens of Nottingham alarmed at Somers' behaviour. He preached and prayed over the boy for three days and nights. He slowly recited one after the other fourteen signs of possession; as he talked of them Somers helpfully showed all the signs, one after the other. The boy behaved for all the world like an encyclopedia of one possessed.

Darrel had big plans for Somers. He boasted he would use him to 'expose all the witches in England' and no doubt make a sackful of gold for himself into the bargain.

He made a start by accusing thirteen women, all from Nottingham. These included Alice Freeman, sister of an alderman and a good woman of excellent character. The innocent blood of these women might now be staining the reputation of English justice if it were not for the action of the local judge who threw Alice Freeman's case out of court and referred Darrel's case to the Bishop of London.

Under the bishop's probing questions the sickening trickery of Darrel's was revealed to an appalled world.

The boy William Somers told how Darrel had taught him to feign these fits. He would use black lead to make his mouth foam. Justice has now been done and John Darrel has been thrown out of the church and put in prison.

Samuel Harsnet told the *London Post and Mail*, 'Let his case be a warning to all rogues who would make a dishonest shilling by sending poor and innocent old women to the gallows as witches.

'The church and the law will not be fooled and you will pay the highest price for your evil trickery.'

LONDON WITCH WATCH

Name: Sarah Griffiths

Witchery: Sarah was suspected of being a witch for a long time because a lot of the children who lived near her had strange fits and visions in which they dreamt of cats. She was finally unmasked by a grocer's boy who jeered at her and with a group of pals chucked her in the river. She floated like a cork. Later Sarah cast a spell on the boy and struck him on the arm. His arm turned green and rotted and fell off. He had hideous fits and visions and eventually died of gangrene.

Verdict: Sarah was committed to Bridewell prison in 1704. After this there is no record of her. Maybe she was really a witch and used her powers to escape. Or maybe she was hanged.

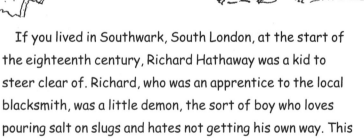

If you lived in Southwark, South London, at the start of the eighteenth century, Richard Hathaway was a kid to steer clear of. Richard, who was an apprentice to the local blacksmith, was a little demon, the sort of boy who loves pouring salt on slugs and hates not getting his own way. This lovable child came up with a tale that made the grown-ups' hair stand on end.

First Richard started having fits and convulsions. Foaming at the mouth he would bark like a dog, burn like fire, vomit pins, nails and lumps of tin. In the midst of this all, through sign language, he indicated that an old woman called Sarah Morduck had bewitched him.

The old lady was brought to him and he scratched her on the face till she bled. After this Richard miraculously recovered for six weeks. Then he fell ill again and fancied drawing a bit more blood.

This time Sarah Morduck was horribly assaulted. One observer reported that 'Her hair and face torn she was kicked, thrown to the ground, stamped on and threatened to be put into a Horse Pond, to be tried by Swimming.'

To save her life Sarah fled to the city of London, where she was followed by a mob – including many children – that jeered at her and threw sticks and stones. But the city was no safer than Southwark. She was hauled up before a local bigwig called Sir Thomas Lane in 1701, who ordered her to be stripped naked. Again Richard was let loose on her to claw as much blood and flesh as he liked.

His antics had made the bloodthirsty boy apprentice quite a celebrity. Prayers were said for him in churches across London and money collected in church boxes. The pickings were rich. He made as much as five or six pounds a time (several hundred pounds in our money).

Meanwhile poor Sarah was condemned as a witch and put into Marshalsea Prison, where she had her first bit of luck. She was tried before Lord Chief Justice Sir John Holt, a kind man who could smell out liars.

Sir John Holt released Sarah Morduck and Richard Hathaway was thrown into Marshalsea in her place as a fraud. But in prison Richard soon had more fits.

So the judge decided to test Richard; another woman was brought to him to scratch and he was told that she was Sarah. He scratched this woman and declared he was better! When he found out his mistake he was struck dumb.

One by one all Richard's little tricks were discovered; he was found to have pins and needles in his pockets. He made the strange noises that seemed to come from nowhere, by scratching his bedposts. He pretended to be starving, while he had bribed a maid to bring him food and drink.

Richard got his just desserts. He was put in prison for a year. And he was also made to stand in the pillory (a sort of wooden frame through which you were locked by the neck and arms) while the enraged citizens of London threw rotten eggs and vegetables at him.

Sarah Morduck was lucky. A hundred years earlier, or with another judge, she might well have been left swinging from the end of a rope while the little imp was acclaimed as the hero of the hour.

CHAPTER NINE

Hellish Nell

The witches and wizards in this book mostly lived in the distant past. They can be left in the pages of history where they are not nearly so spooky.

But self-confessed witches and wizards do exist, even in twenty-first-century London. There are plenty of people who call themselves pagans and practise strange, secret rites.

They may not wear pointy black hats anymore. (Though they may. No one really knows except them.) But they still practise the same rituals and spells as their ancestors did, hundreds of years ago.

Your neighbours could be witches. The postman could be a wizard. Your next door neighbour's cat could be a familiar. Your corner shopkeeper could be a warlock. As you know, after reading this book, it is impossible to tell.

But one thing has changed. The Law doesn't prosecute people for witchcraft anymore. The Witchcraft Act of 1753 was finally repealed in 1951. But it wasn't removed from the statute books before a final, very strange 'witch' was prosecuted under this centuries-old act. Her name was Helen Duncan, and since childhood she had been nicknamed 'Hellish Nell'.

London's Last Witch Trial

DATE: 1944

SCENE: *Courtroom in London's Old Bailey.*

The judge sits in his chair, very grand and dignified in his silver wig and red robes. In front of the judge, sitting in neat rows are the defence and prosecution barristers, their assistants and clerks. The public gallery is thronged with people in shabby wartime clothes. They mutter excitedly and have to be repeatedly shut up by the court officials. Several of the gawpers in the gallery look a bit seedy. All eyes are on the exotic figure in the little wooden witness box. She is Helen Duncan. Duncan is a hefty twenty-two stone, wears a respectable skirt and jacket and has dark hair which has been cut into a neatly curled bob. She looks ordinary enough. But there is a something oddly magnetic about her. When she stands up to speak wheezily a hush descends on the court.

HELLISH NELL: There have been a lot of scoffers in the courtroom, your Lordship. These cynics will be proven wrong. I want to ask permission to prove my powers here.

JUDGE: Powers? I don't understand. What powers?

HELLISH NELL: My psychic powers ... I have been accused of being a fraud. I am told that I can't raise the spirits of the dead. People say that I'm a cheat. Well I'm not. I can speak to the dead and I will prove it. Right here in this witness box.

JUDGE: *(Spluttering a bit)* Outrageous suggestion. Are you proposing to conduct a séance in court?

HELLISH NELL: *(Calmly)* I propose to prove my powers, your Lordship. I wish my powers to be taken in evidence. That's all.

Suddenly a musty odour fills the court, as if yards of old clothes that have been stored in damp and dirt for centuries have been shaken out. The lights start to tremble and Mrs Duncan's wheezing becomes louder. Some members of the public swear that they can see white stuff oozing out of Mrs Duncan's mouths as her eyes start to roll about.

JUDGE: *(Shouting)* Mrs Duncan! What on earth are you up to?

There is pandemonium in the public gallery. Supporters of Duncan start chanting her name. A runty man in a wig bangs an iron collection box with HELEN DUNCAN SUPPORT FUND written on it. The tumult goes on till the judge bangs his gavel (stick) down three times, very hard.

JUDGE: *(Roars)* Silence!! *(He glares at the rabble in the gallery.)* One more peep out of any of you lot and I will have the court cleared. Is that understood?

Silence descends on the court. It is so quiet you can hear Mrs Duncan wheezing.

JUDGE: *(In an icy voice)* Mrs Duncan, stop it immediately.

Suddenly everything goes back to normal. People think they must have imagined the graveyard smell and the lights shaking.

JUDGE: Well, Mrs Duncan, your proposal is something of a precedent. I don't think the Old Bailey has ever had a séance in one of its courtrooms and I don't propose to start right now ... But I will put your suggestion to the prosecution. *(He turns to the prosecution barristers.)* Gentlemen, I will give you one night to consider Mrs Duncan's proposal. We will meet again at the same time tomorrow.

CLERK: All rise.

The judge gets up and walks out of the room. The case is over for the day.

This scene, of which we have imagined the details, is based on fact. Unfortunately, after considering the proposal through the night, the prosecution lawyers refused Mrs Duncan's offer. There never was a séance in an Old Bailey courtroom. Perhaps the lawyers were scared of the scandal which would have resulted, if she had actually managed to raise the spirits of the dead.

After a trial lasting eight days Helen Duncan was found guilty under the Witchcraft Act and sentenced to ten months in Holloway Prison in North London. She was even refused the right to appeal to the House of Lords.

The background to the trial was one of the strangest in the Old Bailey's history. And Mrs Duncan was certainly one of the weirdest characters to have ever appeared in its courtrooms.

Born in Scotland in 1897 Hellish Nell had been marked out as different from early childhood for her tomboyish behaviour and odd predictions . As she grew up she discovered she had weird gifts.

With her husband Henry Duncan, an invalid soldier, acting as her manager, she developed these gifts. In the 1920s she began to hold séances, where she went into a trance. Frothy white stuff called ectoplasm would issue from her mouth and she would be visited by spirits. She would, she said, offer comfort to people by putting them in touch with loved ones who had passed on.

Hellish Nell had two main spirit guides. One was a man called Albert, the other Peggy, a naughty child. Peggy loved to sing 'Baa-Baa Black Sheep' and play little tricks on the people who flocked to Mrs Duncan's séances.

In the early 1930s Mrs Duncan rented a house in Thornton Heath in South London and started holding séances which attracted a crowd of society people. It was around now that her real troubles began when a witch- and ghost-hunter called Harry Price set about to expose her.

He called in doctors to examine her. 'They brought a bag of tools with them,' he wrote, 'and really got down to it. But they found nothing.'

At her next séances these doctors pounced on her ectoplasm and tried to cut it off with surgical scissors. Mrs Duncan became so ill she had to be rushed to St Thomas's hospital where she drank a bottle of disinfectant and had to have her stomach pumped.

In 1933 Mrs Duncan was convicted of fraud. But this didn't put off those who believed in her. Among those who took her powers of talking to the dead seriously were the British Secret Service and the Ministry of Defence. In the desperate days of World War II they began to keep a close watch on Hellish Nell's activities.

In 1941 she conducted a séance where she raised the spirit of a sailor from a warship that had been sunk by German torpedoes. In the brim of his hat she noticed the name of the battle ship, *HMS Barham*.

The government had been trying to hush up the news of *HMS Barham*'s destruction to keep morale high. Rumours that the ship had been lost off the coast of Malta travelled swiftly. The government were shocked and when they were asked by anxious relatives for confirmation, they admitted that the ship had indeed sunk.

The Barham case was the background to Mrs Duncan's arrest in 1944, when plain clothes police officers burst into one of her séances and tried to stop the ectoplasm coming out of her mouth. It is alleged that the real reason that she was arrested was to prevent her revealing details of one of the biggest operations of the war. This was the forthcoming Normandy Landings when Britain and her Allies would land in France to liberate the country from occupation by Nazi Germany.

Mrs Duncan served her time in prison and died of mysterious burns in 1956 – after yet another séance had been broken up by the police.

But Hellish Nell did have some very influential supporters. Britain's wartime leader Winston Churchill sent an angry memo asking why time and money had been wasted on 'obsolete tomfoolery'. But he was known to be interested in the spirits of the dead and had consulted astrologers himself. Churchill visited Duncan in Holloway Prison and while we don't know what was said, we can imagine that the war-time leader and the witch had some interesting things to talk about.

Hellish Nell certainly left her mark on history. When he was re-elected Prime Minister in 1951 Churchill repealed the old Witchcraft Act. Three years later Parliament officially recognized spiritualism – the belief that you can talk to the spirits of the dead – as a religion.

LONDON WITCH WATCH

Name: Joan Petersen, the Witch of Wapping

Imp: A big, black cat.

Witchery: Depends who's asking! Some people say poor old Joan, who was known for prescribing sick people pills and potions, got involved with some nasty plotters who were trying to swindle a lawful heir of his estate. They approached Joan and offered to pay her to say that a Mrs Anne Levington had approached her for poisons to kill a Lady Powell. Joan bravely refused. Then the plotters paid neighbours to accuse Joan of witchcraft. Two women claimed to have been watching by the cradle of a sick child when a black cat appeared from nowhere. One threw a fork at the cat and it vanished. But an hour later it appeared again. The other woman kicked it and immediately her foot blistered and swelled up hugely. Terrified the women abandoned the house and on their way home met the baker, who said that he had seen the strange cat. He swore that it was Joan Petersen, whom he had seen going towards Wapping Island.

Verdict: Hanged at Tyburn in 1652 despite the flimsy evidence.

Witch Wisdom: Test Your Knowledge

1) What was the most common form of execution for witches in Europe?

2)What was the fatal disease that plagued the Middle Ages?

3)Was the Philosopher's Stone real or the product of someone's active imagination?

4) Name one of the accusations Henry VIII levelled at Anne Boleyn to get rid of her.

5) What was the one accessory every witch had to have?

6) What do toads emit when threatened?

7) Which play by Shakespeare has three witches in it?

8) Which English queen was quite soft on wizards and witches?

9) What was a common punishment for forgery in Tudor England?

10) How would you cause a storm at sea and sink the ship of an enemy?

11) What is alchemy?

12) Name two ingredients used to make a witch's love cake.

13) What was the name of the Witchfinder General?

14) When was London's last witch trial?

15) How do you turn your enemies into toads?

Answers

1) Burning at the stake

2) The Black Death (Bubonic Plague)

3) It was real

4) Witchcraft or adultery

5) A familiar

6) A poison curiously called bufagin

7) Macbeth

8) Elizabeth I

9) The chopping off of ears - remember nasty 'skryer' Ned Kelly

10) Throw an enchanted cat into the sea (how you enchant the cat however is another matter)

11) The turning of base metals into gold

12) Choose from: sweat, flour, burnt hair, oil and eggs

13) Mathew Hopkins

14) 1944 - the trial of Hellish Nell

15) Wouldn't you like to know?

93

Other books from Watling St you'll love

CRYPTS, CAVES AND TUNNELS OF LONDON
By Ian Marchant
Peel away the layers under your feet and discover the unseen treasures of London beneath the streets.
ISBN 1-904153-04-6

GRAVE-ROBBERS, CUT-THROATS AND POISONERS OF LONDON
By Helen Smith
Dive into London's criminal past and meet some of its thieves, murderers and villains.
ISBN 1-904153-00-3

DUNGEONS, GALLOWS AND SEVERED HEADS OF LONDON
By Travis Elborough
For spine-chilling tortures and blood-curdling punishments, not to mention the most revolting dungeons and prisons you can imagine.
ISBN 1-904153-03-8

THE BLACK DEATH AND OTHER PLAGUES OF LONDON
By Natasha Narayan
Read about some of the most vile and rampant diseases ever known and how Londoners overcame them – or not!
ISBN 1-904153-01-1

GHOSTS, GHOULS AND PHANTOMS OF LONDON
By Travis Elborough
Meet some of the victims of London's bloodthirsty monarchs, murderers, plagues, fires and famines – who've chosen to stick around!
ISBN 1-904153-02-X

RATS, BATS, FROGS AND BOGS OF LONDON
By Chris McLaren
Find out where you can find some of the creepiest and crawliest inhabitants of London.
ISBN 1-904153-05-4

BLOODY KINGS AND KILLER QUEENS OF LONDON
By Natasha Narayan
Read about royal baddies and their gruesome punishments.
ISBN 1-904153-16-X

HIGHWAYMEN, OUTLAWS AND BANDITS OF LONDON
By Travis Elborough
Take yourself back to the days when the streets of London hummed with the hooves of highwaymen's horses and the melodic sound of 'Stand and deliver!'
ISBN 1-904153-13-5

PIRATES, SWASHBUCKLERS AND BUCCANEERS OF LONDON
By Helen Smith
Experience the pockmarked and perilous life of an average London pirate and his (or her) adventures.
ISBN 1-904153-17-8

REBELS, TRAITORS AND TURNCOATS OF LONDON
By Travis Elborough
What could you expect if you were a traitor – and you were discovered? Take your pick from some of the most hideous punishments ever invented.
ISBN 1-904153-15-1

SPIES, SECRET AGENTS AND SPOOKS OF LONDON
By Natasha Narayan
Look through the spy hole at some of our greatest spies and their exploits, to how to make your own invisible ink.
ISBN 1-904153-14-3

In case you have difficulty finding any Watling St books in your local bookshop, you can place orders directly through

BOOKPOST
Freepost
PO Box 29
Douglas
Isle of Man
IM99 1BQ

Telephone: 01624 836000

email: bookshop@enterprise.net